Investing In Stocks for Beginners

From Zero To Expert

Table of Contents

Introduction 1

Chapter 1: An Introduction to Investments 3

   The Different Types of Financial Investments 3

      Cash Equivalents 3

      Bonds 6

      Stocks 10

      Mutual Funds 24

      Exchange-traded funds (ETFs) 26

      Private investment funds 27

   Choosing the Right Investment for You 27

Chapter 2: The Stock Market 29

   How the Stock Market Works 29

Chapter 3: Getting Started in the Stock Market 31

      1. Know what you want to achieve 31

      2. Straighten out your finances 31

      3. Save up for emergencies 32

      4. Do not quit your job 33

      5. Familiarize yourself with the stock market 33

   Choosing a Stockbroker 35

      1. Suitability to your needs 35

      2. Client protection and insurance 36

3. Consider Minimum deposit amounts and fees 36

4. Trading platform 37

5. Client education 38

6. Ease of transaction with the broker 38

7. Customer service 39

Buying and selling shares of stock 39

Chapter 4: Principles of Investing in the Stock Market 41

Best Practices in Stock Investing 42

1. Start early 42

2. Start with the basics 42

3. Invest regularly 43

3. Invest only in good companies 43

4. Aim for long-term returns 43

5. Diversify stock investments 44

6. Gradually build up your positions 44

7. Continue investing even when there's a crisis 45

8. Adjust when needed 45

Choosing the Right Stocks for Investment 46

1. Earnings 46

2. Price to earnings (P/E) ratio 46

3. Dividend payout and consistency 47

4. Debt ratio 47

Selling Your Stock Investments 48

Chapter 5: Stock Investing Strategies 49
Stock Investing for Income 49
Value Investing 49
Growth Investing 52
Index fund investing 53
Dollar-cost Averaging 54
Averaging down 54

Chapter 6: Principles of Trading in the Stock Market 55
Best Practices in Stock trading 55
   1. Always have a plan and stick to it 55
   2. Do your research 56
   3. Treat it as a business 56
   4. Be a continuous learner 56
   5. Protect your trading capital 56
   6. Do not risk what you can't afford to lose 56
   7. Always use a stop loss 57
   8. Know when to stop 57

Technical Analysis 57
   1. Price trend 57
   2. Chart patterns 58
   3. Moving averages 58
   4. Volume and momentum indicators 59
   5. Oscillators 59

Chapter 7: Stock Trading Strategies 61
    Day Trading 61
    Position Trading 61
    Swing Trading 62
    Scalping 62

Chapter 8: Common Mistakes in Stock Investing and Trading ... 63
    1. Poor Preparation 63
    2. Being Emotional 64
    3. No Recordkeeping 64
    4. Anticipating Returns 65
    5. Dependence on Tools 65

Conclusion 67

Bonus Section! 69

Introduction

This book contains what you need to know to get started in the stock market. It answers almost every question that people ask about it without any hype or promises. It provides practical steps on how you can get started and how you can make good decisions in the stock market.

Although this book only touches upon the basics, it serves as a great introductory material to create a good foundation for learning the more complicated things after. It provides the best practices that traders and investors follow to be successful in the stock market. It even gives the different ways you can approach the stock market that would suit your goals and risk tolerance.

After reading this book, you will be equipped with the needed knowledge to start your journey towards a better financial future. You will know what you need to avoid, so you do not make stupid and costly mistakes. And, lastly, you will increase your chances of achieving the financial goals that would greatly benefit yourself, your family, and your loved ones.

Thanks for downloading this book. I hope you enjoy it!

Chapter 1: An Introduction to Investments

When you invest, you are putting your money on an asset for a potential return in the future. Most of us are only familiar with a bank savings account and the potential return of interest income that comes with it. But, the savings account that you can get from your bank is not the only form of investment out there. It is one of the least favorable investment for you.

This is why it is vital to start learning the different investment vehicles available to you. Although this book is about stock investing, knowing the other options available for you would not hurt. It could even help since these investments are also used by companies to improve their financial standing. Furthermore, knowing the different financial securities can help you better understand the reports and press releases that you would read in researching for your stock investments.

The Different Types of Financial Investments

Cash Equivalents

Cash equivalents are financial instruments that can be considered as cash when accounting for one's assets. These are good as cash due to their ease of being converted to cash. The ease of conversion stems from their nature to being accepted as good as cash or the short time between issuance and maturity date (no longer than less than a year). Examples include treasury bills, commercial paper, and short-term government bonds.

Treasury bills

Also known as T-Bills, treasury bills are debt obligations issued by the government to fund its various projects. These are often sold in set denominations that reach maturity within a year or less. Investors purchase these at a discount and are paid back with the full amount indicated in its issuance. The income received by the investor is considered as the interest income from this investment.

Interest rates are often dictated by how much time the debt obligation reaches its maturity. Longer maturity periods often equate to relatively higher interest rates.

Investors can purchase a treasury bill and hold onto it until maturation to realize interest. They can also sell it in the secondary market before maturity at market price. Prices of treasury bills in the market are influenced by conditions of the country's economy, monetary policy, and general supply and demand.

Treasury bills are among investments that have the lowest risk. It has no risk of the borrower defaulting on the obligation since the government guarantees its payment. However, it only pays a fixed return in the form of interest income and has the lowest interest rate compared to other debt instruments.

Commercial papers

Commercial papers are debt instruments issued by a corporation that usually matures in 270 days or less. It is not tied to collateral and, therefore, makes it a form of short-term unsecured debt. These are issued to acquire financing for payroll, inventory, accounts payable, and payment of short-term liabilities. Like treasury bills, investors buy it at a discount and receive the full price upon maturation.

Only large corporations and banks with an investment-grade rating from Standard & Poor's and Moody's can issue commercial papers. These businesses use it as an alternative to acquiring bank loans that require relatively more tedious documentation and processes and a higher interest rate.

These instruments are often availed by investment firms, mutual funds, and banks. But, retail investors are starting to avail of these opportunities more and more.

Interest rates from commercial papers are usually higher compared to treasury bills and other guaranteed debt instruments. However, due to its nature, these are not covered by deposit insurance.

Marketable securities

Marketable securities are any unrestricted short-term financial instrument issued by a publicly listed company for equity or debt securities. Like the two cash equivalents, these are issued with the intention of funding business activities or expansion.

Marketable securities falling under the classification of cash equivalents are those that mature in less than a year. Aside from instruments with short-term maturity, it also includes financial tools that originally have a maturation period for more than one year but have been purchased in the secondary market when its maturity is in less than a year.

Bonds

Bonds are fixed-income instruments that represent debt borrowed from an investor. A bond is typically an I.O.U. between the investor, acting as the lender, and the borrower. Companies, municipalities, state governments, government agencies, and sovereign governments can issue these fixed income instruments. The funds acquired by the bond issuer can use it to raise funds for projects, refinancing existing debts, or maintain business operations.

Those who hold bonds are considered as creditors of the bond issuer. The initial creditors do not have to hold bonds until maturity. They can sell it to other investors after its issue at a price that other investors will buy. Like stocks, this price is influenced by the supply and demand for the financial instrument.

Basic Characteristics of Bonds

Face value

This is the amount the borrower would return to the creditor upon the maturity of the bond. It is also the value used in calculating interest payments.

Coupon rate

This is the rate that the borrower would pay on top of the bond face value. The coupon rate is paid on an annual basis until the maturity date. The payments can be divided into multiple payments in a year, depending on the terms stated in the bond issued.

Maturity date

This is the date when the bond issuer will pay the face value to the current bondholder.

Time to maturity

This is the amount of time left before the bond matures.

Issue price

This is the original price of the bond when the issuer started selling it.

Chapter 1: An Introduction to Investments

Credit rating

This is the score given by credit agencies, like Moody's and S&P, on the creditworthiness of bond issuers. The rating indicates the possibility of a bond issuer paying back their debt obligations.

Primary Bond Categories

Government bonds

These are issued by the government, which is usually backed by their treasury. Government bonds with less than a year to maturity are called bills, those with 1 to 10 years are called notes, and those with more than 10 years are called bonds. These are also known as sovereign debt.

Corporate bonds

These are issued by companies. Corporate bonds offer more favorable terms and interest rates than bank loans.

Municipal bonds

These are bonds issued by cities, states, counties, and municipalities. Municipal bonds are used to pay for general obligation and fund developments sponsored by the local government. In some cases, the bond is issued as debt on behalf of non-profit hospitals or colleges.

Agency bonds

These bonds are issued by government-affiliated organizations. Agency bonds come in two types – federal government agency bonds and government-sponsored enterprise bonds.

Federal agency government bonds include those issued by the Government National Mortgage Association, Small Business Administration, and the Federal Housing Administration. These bonds are backed by the government's treasury but are less liquid compared to government bonds.

On the other hand, government-owned corporations issue GSE bonds. Examples of such organizations include the Federal National Mortgage Association and Federal Farm Credit Banks Funding Corporation. These are not backed by the government's treasury and, therefore, have a higher coupon rate due to the increased risk.

Different Bond Varieties

Vanilla bonds

These do not have any unusual features. It just has a fixed coupon, a defined maturity date, and issued and redeemed at face value.

Zero-coupon bonds

These bonds do not pay interest payments. Instead, these are issued at a discount. Upon maturity, the issuer pays the creditor at full face value.

Callable bonds

These bonds have an option to be repurchased by the issuer before its maturity. Callable bonds are often bought back when interest rates decrease. When this occurs, issuers buy back the bonds and reissue it with a lower coupon rate.

Puttable bonds

Puttable bonds let bondholders sell the instrument back to the issuer before maturity. This option makes the bond more appealing to creditors since they can get the principal back if the bond might decrease in value or interest rates might increase.

Convertible bonds

These debt instruments have an option to be converted to stock after a specified date. This type of bond is often used when the issuer can only afford a coupon rate.

Floating rate bonds

These bonds do not have a fixed coupon rate. Instead, its rate is linked to a specified interest rate benchmark (like a treasury bond rate).

Stocks

Stocks are a type of investment instrument that represents a portion of a corporation's ownership and the rights that come along with it. A company initiates the sale of stock to raise capital for business growth or expansion. Those purchasing a company's stock are given a portion of the ownership depending on how many units they bought and how this number relates to the number of shares issued by the company.

Ownership of the company's stock gives an investor the right to receive a portion of the business' profits. They also have voting rights in proportion to the percentage of the company's shares they own when it comes to board membership and other business decisions requiring input from stockholders.

Holders of a company's stock have limited liability on the company's obligations. This prevents debtors and regulators from chasing after the assets of a company's investors when the business becomes bankrupt and still has outstanding debt. The worst that can happen to investors on this financial instrument is the complete loss of their investment due to its shares losing value.

"Shares" and "stocks" are often used interchangeably when referring to this financial instrument. The word "stock" is used when referring to shares of a certain company or to the financial instrument. On the other hand, "shares" is used as a unit of measurement when referring to a particular amount of the instrument.

The Difference between a Private Company and a Public Company

When people think of stocks, they immediately look to companies listed in the various stock exchanges like the NYSE. But, shares of stock are not unique to these companies. As long as a company is a corporation, it has shares issued to its investors or owners that serve as proof of their ownership.

Those listed in exchanges are called publicly-held companies. They are called as such since investing in them is available to the public. Therefore, a portion of its ownership is already held by the public.

On the other hand, unlisted corporations are known as privately-held companies. The investors in these businesses are limited to a small group that often involve the founders, venture capitalists, private investors, and management. People often mistake such companies as small. But, this is not necessarily the case since some of the biggest companies in America and the world are privately-held.

Private companies and public companies have distinct differences, especially in regards to investments. If you are looking to go beyond the stock exchange in investing, it is important that you are aware of these things.

Private companies

> They cannot sell stocks or bonds in the public market to raise funds or capital.
>
> They have a smaller number of investors and, therefore, receive fewer demands from shareholders.
>
> They are not required to disclose financial information to the public or the Securities and Exchange Commission.

They have a limited source of funds to fund expenses or expansions.

Public companies

They opened the whole, or a portion of, ownership of the company for public investment, which gives them access to more investors but opens themselves to more decision-making input due to the greater number of shareholders.

They can turn to financial markets for funding by selling stocks or bonds.

They are required to file earnings reports to the SEC on a quarterly basis, which are made available to the public.

How Stocks Earn

Stock prices of publicly listed companies rise and fall depending on the supply and demand present for the stock. You can earn when you buy shares of stock and sell it at a higher price. Earnings that arise from such an action are called as capital gain.

You can also earn from dividends. Dividends are a company's distribution of its earnings to its shareholders. The board of directors decides on this amount and is divided by the number of outstanding shares of the company.

There are two types of dividends – cash and stock. Cash dividends are cash payments made to shareholders via check or electronic transfer. The amount is either an amount per share or a percentage of a stated stock price. Cash dividends using the latter would result in a loss equivalent to the percentage paid to shareholders.

On the other hand, stock dividends result in an increase in the shares that a company's shareholders hold. This would be expressed in a percentage so, if a 5% stock dividend is announced and you own 50 shares, you would receive 2.5 shares. A stock dividend would result in a decreased share price since the total number of outstanding shares increased.

Types of Stock

1. Common stock

This is the financial security that entails ownership in a corporation. Common stockholders exercise this ownership by voting on members of the board of directors and on corporate policies. They are the lowest priority when distributing the company's assets in the event of its liquidation.

2. Preferred stock

Preferred stocks combine the investment features of equity and debt. Each unit of preferred stock can increase or decrease in price while, at the same time, providing fixed dividends at a fixed rate or following an interest rate benchmark. It is treated with greater preference over common stockholders when it comes to distributing the company's profits or liquidated assets. However, holders of preferred stock have little to no voting rights for electing members of the board or decisions concerning corporate policy.

Important Terms in the Stock Market

The stock market and the practice of investing in it has its own terms. To better equip yourself for success, you have to familiarize yourself with words used by stock market experts, brokers, and investors.

Exchange

A place wherein different investments, including stocks and bonds, are traded between investors and businesses.

OTC market

Over-the-counter market is where trading is done directly between different parties without the supervision of an exchange.

Market trend

This is the perceived direction of where a market is seen to move in the future.

Bull market

The conditions in the market lead to the value and/or price of securities to an increase or, at least, an expected increase for extended periods. These periods can last for months or years. A bull market is characterized by a strong economy, low unemployment rates, high stock demand, high IPO activity, and high investor confidence.

Bear market

The conditions in the market lead to the value and/or price of securities to a decrease. A decrease in prices is only considered a bear market when prices decrease by at least 20% or more from the market's recent high. This is characterized by a widespread negative sentiment among investors.

Broker

An individual or organization facilitating transactions between buyers and sellers of security. Each transaction is charged with a commission, usually on the part of the seller, in exchange for their service. Most stockbrokers provide market research and data for their customers.

Stock index

It provides a market and performance overview of a section of the stock market. An index is calculated through the weighted average of a selection of stocks that best represent its section. Indices are available in terms of geography (global or regional), industry (NYSE Arca Pharmaceutical Index), income level (developed markets), nation (S&P 500 and FTSE 100), individual exchanges (NYSE US 100 and Nikkei 225), and groups of exchanges (OMX Nordic 40).

IPO

This is the first sale of a company's stock to the public.

Secondary offering

This is the sale of previously withheld shares by a publicly-listed company to the market.

Blue chip stocks

These are stocks from large and industry-leading corporations. These companies pay significant dividends and have a reputation for sound financial management.

Value stocks

These stocks trade at a market price below what their earnings, sales, and dividends show. Value stocks usually have low price-to-earnings ratio and price-to-book ratios.

Growth stocks

These stocks are of high quality and are expected to have above-average growth compared to the rest of the market. Growth stocks have high price-to-earnings and price-to-book ratios.

Large-cap stocks

These are stocks that reach a market capitalization of $10 billion or more.

Small-cap stocks

These are stocks that have a market capitalization of $300 million to $2 billion

Mid-cap stocks

These are the stock that has a market capitalization more than small-cap stocks but below large-cap stocks.

Penny stocks

These are stocks that trade for less than $5 per share in a stock exchange or the OTC market. These stocks have high price volatility in a single trading day.

Ticker symbol

It is an arrangement of characters that serve as a unique identifier for publicly traded stocks. These are also used for indices, options, bonds, and mutual funds.

Quote

This is the latest trading price of a stock. A stock quote is more up-to-date when found in a broker's stock trading platform.

Capitalization

This is how much the market thinks a company is worth.

Authorized shares

This is the total number of shares that a company has.

Public float

This is the number of shares that a company makes available for trade in the stock market.

Market price

This is how much was paid for each share of stock in the latest order executed. This will fluctuate every time the price changes in the market. The market price upon closing the market for the day is the one recorded in the charts.

Target price

This is the price of a stock projected in the future by an investment analyst. The target price is estimated using a combination of analysis of a stock's finances, future supply and demand in the market, fundamentals, and technical data. The target price is the ideal point for some investors and traders to sell their position and realize their gains.

Fundamental analysis

This is the process of looking at the financial health of a business and the external factors affecting it. It examines important business ratios involving the company's assets, revenue, liabilities, and management, the state of the industry, and the current economic and political situation in its country, region, and the world.

Technical analysis

This is the examination of current and past price movements to identify previous patterns in the market. This pattern is used to create a forecast of future price movements of a stock traded in the market.

Buy

This means that you intend to buy shares or take a position in a company's stock.

Sell

This means that you intend to sell a given number of a company's stock.

Ask

This is the price per share that people want to get in exchange for their stock.

Bid

This is the price that people are willing to pay for each share to get a stock.

Bid-ask spread

This is the difference between how much people are willing to pay for each share of stock and how much people are willing to sell for each.

Yield

This is the return on investment received from a stock investment in terms of dividends. This is calculated by dividing the stock's annual dividend amount by the amount paid for its purchase.

High

It refers to the highest price point that a stock experienced for its all-time record or for a given period.

Low

It refers to the lowest price point that a stock experienced for its all-time record or for a given period.

Moving average

It is the average price per share of a stock during a certain timeframe. Common timeframes are in 50 and 200 days.

Volume

It is the number of stock traded for a specific time period, usually daily. It can also mean the number of total shares purchased of a stock.

Volatility

It is a measure of a security or market's variance in price within a given timeframe. A stock with higher volatility would have dramatic price changes within a short time. Lower stock volatility would illustrate a steadier stock price.

Chapter 1: An Introduction to Investments

Beta

This measures the relationship of a stock's price to the movement of the market, usually the exchange where it is traded. A beta of 2 means that the stock moves 2 points for every 1 point of movement of the whole market.

Position

It is a single stock that an investor or trader owns. When one says that he has four positions, this means that they own four different stocks.

Position size

This is how much money they have invested in a single stock.

Order

This is a bid to buy or sell shares of stock or option contracts.

Market order

It is the instruction provided that will be immediately executed at the current market price of a stock. It is always fulfilled as long as willing buyers and sellers are present.

Limit order

It is an instruction given to a broker to buy or sell a stock at a specified price or better.

Day order

This is an order that only lasts until trading closes for the day.

GTC order

A good-till-cancelled order stands even when the market closes and will only be executed when the market price meets the indicated bid or ask price.

Stop-loss order

It is a conditional order executed when a security reaches the indicated price. Once it reaches the indicated price, it becomes a market order. It is designed to limit losses or protect profits incurred from a position.

Limit order

It is a conditional order executed when a security reaches a specified price or better. This helps a buyer to ensure that they get in or out of the position at the pre-determined market price of the stock.

Stop-limit order

It is a conditional order that combines elements of stop-loss and limit order. The order is executed at a specified price within a certain timeframe. But, this will only occur when the given stop price occurs in the market.

The stop-limit order provides a trader control on when the order would be executed. However, it has no guarantee of occurring since the stock may not reach the stop price within the specified timeframe.

Mutual Funds

Mutual funds are financial vehicles that consist of pooled funds that are invested in a mixture of financial securities and assets. This could be a combination of stocks, bonds, money market instruments, and more. Fund managers manage these funds by allocating the capital into different instruments with varying volatility. This strategy is known as diversification and helps in maximizing long-term returns while helping manage exposure to risk.

Mutual funds provide investors with limited capital to access investments requiring capital that they do not have. Each investor holds shares in the fund and experiences the proportionate gains or losses incurred by the fund. The performance of the mutual fund is based on the changes in its total market capitalization.

Mutual Fund Shares Explained

To invest in a mutual fund, you would have to buy a share in it. However, buying a mutual fund is different from purchasing shares of stock. There is no market price for these shares. Instead, the price is the total value of the securities in the fund divided by the total number of outstanding mutual fund shares. This value is known as the net asset value (NAV) or net asset value per share (NAVPS).

To realize your gains from the investment, you do not have to sell your shares. All you have to do is to redeem them, and the funds will be settled by the end of the trading day.

Aside from price fluctuations of the securities it holds, a mutual fund also earns income from the stock dividends and bond interest payments held in its portfolio. The income can be distributed to fund shareholders, or added to the capital to increase NAVPS.

Types of Mutual Funds

There are several types of mutual funds available. Each are created to create funds that cater to the different securities available for investment, and to the varying investment objectives among investors.

Money market funds

These funds invest in short-term fixed-income investments such as bonds, commercial paper, and certificates of deposit. These have a greater return compared to bank deposits but have a lower potential return compared to other funds.

Bond funds

These funds invest in fixed income instruments such as government bonds and investment-grade or high-yield corporate bonds. These generate an income from interest and have a greater return than money market funds while having a less volatile NAVPS than stock funds.

Stock Funds

These mutual funds hold a variety of publicly traded stocks. The stocks held depend on a fund's investment goal. It could aim for dividend income and capital gain through blue-chip stocks or more aggressive growth through value and growth stocks.

Index Funds

These funds have the objective of tracking the performance of an index. It has lower administrative fees since fund managers do not do much work since they only have to create a portfolio that resembles the components of the benchmarked index.

Balanced funds

These funds mix fixed-income and stock securities. This results in a greater potential return than bond funds while decreasing the volatility of stock funds. A balanced fund can lean towards more potential growth by adding more equities in its assets or more conservative risk by allocating more to bonds.

Exchange-traded funds (ETFs)

These are similar to index funds in the fact that these track an index by holding a combination of securities. But, unlike mutual funds tracking indices, ETFs are easily traded in exchanges through market prices similar to stocks. It also provides more transparency than a mutual fund since its holdings are disclosed each day. Lastly, taxes are only paid upon selling the investment.

Private investment funds

These are funds that do not allow investment from retailer investors or the public. Private investment funds use aggressive investment strategies that public funds would immediately avoid due to unreasonable exposure to risk. Examples of a private investment fund are hedge funds and private equity funds.

Choosing the Right Investment for You

Any kind of investment that has a potential for earning you income or increasing your capital entails a risk of losing the amount invested. Furthermore, the more potential for returns means the greater the risk of losing the capital invested in the asset.

This is especially true for stocks. Equities have great potential for increasing the invested capital. This potential return has an equal potential to turn as a potential loss. This is the nature of things since the trend of stock's price can increase or decrease just the same.

This is why you must first know your risk tolerance before investing in any asset. Risk tolerance is how much risk you are willing to take and able to bear. Investing in something with the risk that you are uncomfortable with will make increase your chances of making poor decisions. Taking on too much risk makes it easier for you to make mistakes in selling or buying a position.

Chapter 1: An Introduction to Investments

The easiest way to determine if you took on too much risk is with how your investments are affecting your mind. If you are having trouble sleeping with how much you are thinking about your investments and fearing how a downtrend can affect your portfolio. You can prevent this by answering tests designed to assess your risk tolerance before you even go into investing. These tests will help you determine how much risk you can stomach from your investments.

Chapter 2: The Stock Market

The stock market is a place where individuals and organizations can buy and sell shares of stock available for public investment. It can refer to the general market that buys and sell shares or to a specific stock market such as the New York Stock Exchange, Nasdaq, Japan Exchange Group, and Shanghai Stock Exchange. The stock market is often a critical component to a country's economic development since it gives companies quick access to capital, and investors a place for investing their assets.

How the Stock Market Works

Most stocks are traded in the various stock exchanges in the world. These exchanges are regulated by the government agencies responsible for securities and exchange in the countries hosting these exchanges. The government agencies protect those investing in the publicly listed companies from financial fraud and help maintain the operation of the stock exchanges.

There are three major players in the stock market – the investment banks, stockbrokers, and investors. The investment banks are responsible for handling the initial public offering of companies when they decide to offer their shares for public investment. These banks are approached by these companies and become their underwriters. As an underwriter, the investment bank will use its research on the company to determine the guaranteed minimum price per share and how much of the ownership the company is willing to relinquish to the public as shares. In return, the investment bank handles the initial issue of shares to the public for a fee. Usually, large institutional investors, like mutual fund companies, purchase shares sold during an IPO. After that, all trading of the shares occurs in the stock exchange – the secondary market.

In the exchange, stockbrokers buy and sell the stocks according to the order of their clients – the investors. Stockbrokers might also act as financial advisors, so their clients make the best decisions according to their goals. They often offer research on publicly traded companies and provide a forecast on overall market index or stock price performance. This service is offered since stockbrokers want their clients to succeed in their investments and trades. If they experience success in their stock trades, they will more likely transact more trades and remain as their customer.

Chapter 3: Getting Started in the Stock Market

Getting started in the stock market requires the same considerations before getting started investing in any type of asset. You must first check your financial situation and identify your goals.

1. Know what you want to achieve

What you can do with the stock market depends on what you want to achieve out of it. Are you aiming to use it as a means to replace your income and quit your job? Are you going to use it to build wealth alongside your job? Are you going to use it to build-up funds for retirement?

Each of these goals would require a different approach to the stock market compared to the other two. For example, replacing the income from your work would require a more aggressive strategy than a strategy for building up your wealth or retirement fund. This also applies to the frequency of trades that you would be doing within the week.

2. Straighten out your finances

You must consider your job security, your income, any outstanding debt, and other financial obligations you have, your current and future expenses, your cash savings, and your

Chapter 3: Getting Started in the Stock Market

household budget. This will give you a good picture of your finances that will help you make a more informed decision if you have the budget to get started now. If not, you can build up capital for the stock market with your job. Either way, you will have a better starting point and will not put in money that you cannot afford.

Knowing your financial situation will also help you keep track of your expenses moving forward. It can help prevent unnecessary expenses that might negatively affect your funds for trading or, worse, cause you to take on debt.

3. Save up for emergencies

Before you even get started, you need to save money for emergencies. You will not put this into investments that have the risk of loss in value or capital. The most that you can do with this money is to put it in a money market fund or certificates of deposits.

The amount should be enough to provide for at least three months of your living expenses. This will be crucial in the event that you lose your job, experience a health emergency, or any other unexpected financial emergencies. Having this fund is crucial in preventing yourself from taking on losses in your investment in the event of such emergencies occur.

4. Do not quit your job

The worst mistake that you can do when starting out in the stock market is quitting your job. It is easy to get carried with how much earning potential the stock market has in store for anyone. But, before you even get to that point, you will have to learn the ropes first and gain enough experience to create good results. And, as they say, the only way to get that experience is by doing, which comes with making mistakes. This could mean losing money depending on your strategy and falling short in terms of achieving goals in time or on target.

Having a job will help maintain a sense of security in terms of your finances. This sense of security will help you maintain a mental balance in the midst of the ups and downs of your investments, your losses in your trading capital, and the expected losses any beginner will experience. Going through these without a regular source of income can be difficult mentally and could affect investing decisions. It could even spill over to other aspects of your life.

5. Familiarize yourself with the stock market

You are already doing this by reading this book. This book presents you with the basics that you need to know to get started and answers the frequently asked question about it. But, there is a lot more than you can do.

You can get a better start in the stock market by learning from successful stock investors and traders. You can find books by authors who already went through what you will be going through. You will essentially learn from their experiences, successes, and failures, which will help you achieve your goals faster. Some of the best books go beyond how to do research, create strategies, or make a trade, and include the psychological aspects of trading in the stock market. Some good books are the following:

> The Intelligent Investor by Benjamin Graham
>
> One Up On Wall Street by Peter Lynch
>
> Mastering The Trade by John Carter
>
> The Disciplined Trader: Developing Winning Attitudes by Mark Douglas
>
> The Truth About Day Trading Stocks by Josh DiPetrio
>
> As you are doing this, you can practice making trades with a stock market simulator. This is essentially you testing and playing around the stock market with actual and real-time market events. But, you are not using any money, so it is the best way to apply what you learn in this book. Using a stock simulator is the best way to practice what you just learned and gain a bit of confidence in using the interface used for trading in the stock market.

Choosing a Stockbroker

You cannot trade or invest in the stock market if you can't buy or sell shares in the stock market. To do so, you would have to set-up an account with a stockbroker that will facilitate these transactions for you. Like any service provider, not all stockbrokers are equal. You would want a broker that can provide you the best service without charging you over-the-top fees. Here are the considerations you must take when choosing your broker:

1. Suitability to your needs

You know your objectives in regards to buying and selling shares in the stock market. Therefore, you have an idea of how you would be doing your transactions in regard to trying to achieve these objectives. Brokers would have different features, and it is important that your choice can provide what you require. Important features to consider include charts, financial data, analyst support, educational resources, broker assistance, and customer service channels.

You have to consider if the broker would let your trade in the stock exchanges that you are planning to enter. If you intend to invest in investments other than stock, you might also want to consider brokers that offer the securities you want. Some brokers can provide access to cash equivalents, bonds, and funds for those seeking a one-stop venue for investments. On the other hand, there are those providing access to commodities, options,

Chapter 3: Getting Started in the Stock Market

forex, and other high-risk and specialty asset classes for more advanced investors.

Lastly, you would have to consider your knowledge and experience. Some brokers are beginner-friendly by providing a simple platform for executing stock trades. But, some users prefer a broader range of investment that might confuse those that are just starting out.

2. Client protection and insurance

You have to make sure that the broker you choose follows the law and provides protection for its clients. It should have a relevant regulatory body (such as FINRA in the United States) to authorize its operations to ensure that it provides a fair and honest service to investors. The broker should also provide investor protection insurance for customer cash claims, and deposit insurance for deposit products in the event that the company fails. They should also protect your personal information in their systems, and offer two-factor log-in authentication. Lastly, the broker should have a form of guarantee protection that will reimburse losses caused by fraudulent activities.

3. Consider Minimum deposit amounts and fees

Most stockbrokers require a minimum deposit to open an account. A basic stock trading account will typically require a minimum balance of $500 to $1,000. But, if you want to open a margin account, you would have to prepare a relatively higher amount and must consider their interest rate for making a trade on margin.

As for fees, you must be careful of brokers that advertise fees that seem too good to be true. Check the fine print in the agreement and see if there are any hidden and additional fees.

Lastly, brokers generate revenue from the commission fees charged on your trades. These are often charged in two ways – on the volume of your trade or on the frequency of your trades. You would have to choose the broker that works best with how you would choose to buy and sell shares.

4. Trading platform

If you can, test the platform before you start using the broker to buy and sell shares. It does not matter if it's a web-based or app-based. What you are looking for is a platform that lets you place an order smoothly. It should let you trade the securities that you need to trade and create orders that you require for your goals and schedule.

The trading platform should also provide real-time data. You should be able to set-up watchlists and alerts so you can get notifications, preferably via text. You should also consider if you would require trading in extended hours and if the broker would charge extra for it.

Take a look at the charting features available on the platform. See if it plots the data that you want to see and if you find it easy to do so. Do not settle for a broker that lack any of the basic indicators - volume, simple moving averages, RSI, Bollinger bands, stochastics, and MACD.

Lastly, you should find it easy to use the brokerage's platform. It should only take you more than 30 minutes to get used to browsing the different menus and pages and grasp how to create and execute trade orders. At the very least, the broker should provide a short video tutorial on using the platform.

5. Client education

Even if you can find the generic and basic information in this book and other sources online, brokers are a valuable source of information for stock trading. Market updates and fundamental data can provide great insight from experts that will equip you to create better decisions. Of course, this depends on the quality and capability of their sources and staff.

6. Ease of transaction with the broker

It is important that you can easily add or withdraw money from your brokerage account. Delays and long turnaround times can make you miss sudden opportunities even if you schedule your deposits regularly. Moreover, you should choose a broker that will let you add or withdraw funds with the methods available to you – bank or wire transfer, debit or ATM card, or linked bank accounts.

7. Customer service

Choose a broker that provides access to customer service quickly and easily. This is even more important when you are just starting out and require additional assistance in the beginning. Check if they provide the customer service channel that you prefer.

Buying and selling shares of stock

Once you have an account with a broker, you can start buying stocks in an exchange. There is no minimum to how much you have to buy to invest in a stock. But, it is best to buy in lots since there are charges added on top of the investment you are making. This is why it is advised to purchase at least a single lot size for a given stock.

A lot is a fixed increment that stocks are traded in the market. These increments often come in 100s while higher-priced stocks come in 10s. You can still set orders with an increment below the number of lots for the stock since companies can split shares or issue stock dividends.

Trades are created through the orders entered in the order entry interface of your broker's platform. These orders indicate the stock and number of shares that you want to buy, and the ask or bid price for each share. Once you submit your order in your broker's order entry interface, the broker will facilitate this for

Chapter 3: Getting Started in the Stock Market

you electronically. Orders will push through when there are matching sell and bid orders in the market.

When the orders push through, buyers receive their new shares and have the cost of the shares and the associated fees deducted from their accounts. For sellers, the broker deducts the relevant fees from the proceeds before crediting what remains to the seller's account.

What you earn from stocks sold that increase in price is subject to tax. The rate would depend on how long you held the stock. If you held the stock for more than a year, the proceeds would be subject to long-term capital gains rates depending on your taxable income. But, if you held it for less than a year, the proceeds would be subjected to ordinary income tax rates depending on your taxable income.

Chapter 4: Principles of Investing in the Stock Market

Investing is a means to build wealth in the long-term through financial securities. Stock investing is the most popular strategy to accomplish this. This popularity arises from the fact that stocks provide greater returns in the long-term (5 to 10 years) compared to bank deposits, money market instruments, and fixed-income investments. Moreover, although there is no guarantee in the future performance of any investment, the stock market as a whole has an average annual return of 10 percent since 1926. This performance takes into account the short-term volatility, rapid price changes, and historic double-digit price crashes in the stock market.

Investing can also help your savings maintain, and even exceed, its purchasing power in the midst of inflation. This makes stock investing ideal not only for helping you save up for retirement. But, it can also help you save up for big-ticket expenses, like a new house or a college education, that will be spent after, at least, 5 years in the future.

Chapter 4: Principles of Investing in the Stock Market

Best Practices in Stock Investing

1. Start early

In any type of investment, starting early would always be the best if you want to experience greater returns. This is the same case with investing in stocks. Having more time between your start and the time that you would need your returns would give you a higher return from your investment. For example, if you intend to use your investment for your retirement, starting at the age of 25 would give you more years in the stock market that your capital is invested compared to starting at 35 years of age. So, if you started with $25,000 and have that compounded with the annual average of 10% per year, you would have a total investment value of $543,000 if you started at 25 years, and a total of $215,000 if you started at 35.

2. Start with the basics

The stock market can be overwhelming with the different approaches that you can do, and the various ways that you can invest or trade stocks. But, even if some guru would praise some sophisticated approach, you do not have to do it since a lot of investors succeeded by just sticking to the basics. In fact, if you are a beginner, it is advised to start with a low-cost fund that tracks a valuable index like the S&P 500. You could even make do with this fund if you prefer a hands-off approach to your stock investments.

3. Invest regularly

Regular annual or monthly investments into more shares will give you a greater return from your investment in the end. This is due to a regular increase in funds available for purchasing more stocks and the compounding effect returns on your investment. Using the same conditions from the previous example, if one person would only invest $25,000 once while another would invest $25,000 per year, the latter would have $7,000,000 by the end compared to the other's $543,000.

3. Invest only in good companies

If you are investing in the stock market, you have to invest in great companies listed for public investment. You want to look for companies with great potential, as seen from their finances. As an investor, you are in it for the long haul, and you will get the most returns if you focus on valuable companies. Depending on your strategy, these companies would either be value or growth stocks that have great capital gain potential or blue-chip stocks with excellent dividend potential. Finding out which companies would give you what you want would require research through fundamental analysis. In most cases, these companies are current, or emerging leaders in their industry or already have great financial performance.

4. Aim for long-term returns

The market prices of any stock in the market will always be volatile in the short term. Events in the company's business and industry, and country's (or the world's) economy will cause stock prices to shoot up or crash down. But, these short-term price fluctuations do not matter if you are implementing a long-term investment plan. If you will look at the long-term trend of a stock market index, the trend is always on the rise since any downturn would have highs that surpass previous ones after 3 to 5 years.

5. Diversify stock investments

Diversification of your investments would always minimize your risk. Although the advice is on spreading your capital on different investment types, the same concept applies even if all your investments are in the stock market. Placing all your capital in one stock would make you more susceptible to changes in the market price and to the risk of losing all your investment.

Even if you are invested in more than one stock, there could still be a lack of diversification in your portfolio. Check if you are holding stocks of the same industry or from the same parent or group of companies. It only takes one event in that sector or that group to affect the whole or majority of your portfolio. This also applies if you are only investing in the stock market of one country or region.

6. Gradually build up your positions

Avoid going all-in in stock even if it is a value stock. You still have no assurance of how the prices will go between its current market price and real value. Also, there is still a possibility that the company experiences a crisis that changes its value that will fall below the current price. Gradual purchases of its shares will prevent you from exposing your capital to this risk. Moreover, this will leave you with more funds to invest in other stocks to help diversify your stock portfolio.

7. Continue investing even when there's a crisis

Your regular investments should continue even when there is a crisis. It is easy to think that you should sell all your investments when there is a financial crisis or a current scare in the economy. But this is the worst thing that you can do. If you did your research well and invested in a good company and this company remains as such even during the present crisis, you have nothing to worry about. The decrease, possibly a rapid one, in market price is more probably due to day traders and emotional sellers reacting to the current events.

In fact, taking out your investments from a good company is the worst thing that you can do. You would more likely be selling the shares of a good company at a loss. Moreover, continuing your investment would even be helpful in the long run since you are essentially buying a valuable stock as if it's on sale.

8. Adjust when needed

The performance of any stock or market is not set in stone. Situations may change, or events may occur that will make what you previously know irrelevant. When this happens, you have to make adjustments to your positions. This is normal, and sticking to a position when the situation has already change would only lead to further losses.

Choosing the Right Stocks for Investment

As mentioned, investing in the stock market requires choosing companies of good quality. You can see which ones are great investments based on indicators in their financial statements. Here are the most important indicators that identify if a stock is a good investment or not:

1. Earnings

The profitability of the company is the most basic indicator if a business is doing well. A stock will have a higher value if it is generating good profits. A company's value is not necessarily equivalent to the market price of its stock. It can either be undervalued, which makes it a great investment opportunity or a value, which can make it as a stock to watch if the market price falls below its actual value.

2. Price to earnings (P/E) ratio

This is the ratio between the share price and the company's annual income. You can find this in financial websites featuring stock information.

If a stock's P/E ratio is higher than the current P/E ratio in the market, the stock is considered trading at or above its current value. But, this does not automatically make the stock a bad investment, especially if it is a low-cap stock with a rapid rate of growth. On the other hand, if it is lower than the market's P/E ratio, it is currently trading below value, which makes it a potential value stock.

3. Dividend payout and consistency

Stocks that show consistent dividend payments and increase make for great income-generating equity investments. Furthermore, regular dividend payments and increases show that the business is growing and financially stable. The best timeframe in analyzing dividend payouts is the stock's dividend payout history for the past 5 to 10 years.

4. Debt ratio

The debt ratio is the proportion between a company's total liabilities and total assets. A higher debt ratio indicates a greater possibility of a company failing to pay its obligation. The ideal debt ratio is 0.4 or lower, while it is best to stay away from stocks with a 0.6 debt ratio.

Stocks that show good indicators have the potential to be suitable investments. But, this potential does not mean that you should invest in them now. You must first determine if these stocks can increase in value or provide dividends to justify committing your capital. A good measure is if it can help you build an average annual return of 12 percent (after taxes) from your stock portfolio. But, if you are only investing in an index fund, the most that you can aim for is 7 percent per year.

Moreover, if you want to maximize the returns that you can get from stock investing, you would want to focus more on value and growth stocks and less on high-cap stocks that generate regular dividend income. Most high-cap stocks with dividend-generating income have a lower growth potential compared to value and growth stocks.

Selling Your Stock Investments

Your strategy for stock investing dictates when you should sell a position. If you are aiming for regular dividend income, holding a position takes priority over realizing your capital gains by selling it. On the other, if your objective is to build wealth by realizing capital gains, you would sell when a position hits its price target.

The price target can be computed by multiplying a stock's P/E ratio at the time of your purchase by 2.3. This results in the expanded P/E ratio, which you would compare with the earnings estimate of the following year. The value that you would get is the price target of the stock.

Knowing a stock's price target is crucial if you want to maximize your earning potential and to make the most of the time with your investment. This is why calculating the price target should be done while you are doing research on good stock investments. Once you have determined a stock's price target, you can then decide if it is worthwhile by subtracting the potential taxes and fees that you would have to pay in the future.

Chapter 5: Stock Investing Strategies

Stock investing is the act of profiting from the stock market over the long-term. Because of this, strategies used for investing prioritize long-term gains. Here are the different ways that investors use to profit over time:

Stock Investing for Income

Stock market investing is mostly about realizing growth from investment by buying and selling stock positions known as an equity portfolio. But, some investors prefer or are looking to add an income from their stock portfolio, which is known as a dividend portfolio. These individuals prioritize stocks paying regular cash dividends.

Since most of these stocks are often more expensive compared to others, it is best to take advantage of bear markets when creating a dividend portfolio. This portfolio should consist of 10 to 30 blue-chip stocks paying regular high dividend income. Moreover, instead of buying and selling stocks for 5 to 10 years, the stocks are purchased and held to build a portfolio generating the investor's income target.

Value Investing

Value investors are shopping for stocks at a bargain with the intention of selling it at its value in the future. This strategy is

Chapter 5: Stock Investing Strategies

founded upon the idea that there is a degree of irrationality in the market. This irrationality creates the scenario for value investors to find stocks being sold at a discounted price. When these discounted stocks realize their value, the investor would then sell them off and earn through capital gain.

This strategy is based on the concept that investors should buy businesses and not the stock. All considerations on investment decisions are based on the state of the business. Stock market prices are just a gauge of how much an investor can potentially earn when the market realizes a business' real worth.

The following are the fundamental indicators that help determine a stock's value:

> **Book value:** Also known as intrinsic value, this is the calculated value of an asset – the company, in the case of stocks. Although it is merely an estimate, it can help identify how the market values a stock. If the price is below the intrinsic value, it is undervalued and a good pick for value investing. It is equivalent to the difference between a company's assets and liabilities (assets – liabilities = book value). If you divide the intrinsic value by the number of outstanding shares, you will have a value that you can compare with the company's stock price.
>
> **Price-to-book (P/B) ratio:** It compares the value of a company's assets against its stock price. It is calculated by

dividing the stock price by the book value per share. If the resulting ratio is more than the stock price, it means that the stock is trading below the company's real value. Unfortunately, the P/B ratio should not be used by itself. A company's book value is easily distorted by recent acquisitions and write-offs, and share buybacks. The book value also fails to show a company's value if it recently went through a period of negative earnings.

Price-to-earnings (P/E) ratio: It helps determine the value of the company to its stock price. A high P/E ratio (more than 1) indicates that the stock is priced above the company's actual value or growth in earnings is expected in the future. Essentially, the ratio shows how much the market is willing to pay per dollar of the company's earnings.

Free cash flow (FCF): It represents the cash generated by the company after subtracting the cash outflows. This shows how much cash the company can make available for creditors and investors at the moment. This is computed but analyzing the FCF over a period of time using a chart will be more useful. If FCF is stable for the past 3 to 5 years, it means that any positive trends in the stock price are less likely to be disrupted in the future.

Value investing requires you to see valuable stocks that are trading below their current book value. These are undervalued by the market due to a lack of information or the usual sentiment of the market. This means that you will have to go against the majority even if the prices drop in the future. As long as your information and calculations are sound, you will benefit from your position. Of course, any new information should be taken into account with your calculations and position.

Growth Investing

Growth investing involves looking at stocks owned by companies that have shown consistent growth and substantial profit in the past. Contrary to value investing, this strategy does not pay heed if the stock is trading above a business's intrinsic value. In the eyes of the growth investor, the company has shown continued growth, and the intrinsic value would eventually follow, which makes the stock still a good investment.

To find good stock investments for this strategy, the following metrics are used:

> **Earnings per share (EPS):** This is calculated by dividing the net earnings available to common shareholders by the number of average outstanding shares of a given period of time. This helps compare a stock to other dividend-paying stocks. It also helps to check the historical data of a stock's EPS to see if the company increases the profit distributed to shareholders.

Profit margin: This is calculated by dividing net revenue with total sales. Higher and stable historical profit margins indicate that a company manages its finances well and shows promise in doing so in the future.

Return on equity (ROE): This is the net income divided by shareholders' equity. The present ROE is compared to the company's average ROE for the past five years. A stable or increasing ROE is indicative of good management practices that result in good returns and efficient business operations.

Stock performance: A good growth stock investment has shown an increase in price at 15 percent in the past year or 100 percent for the past five years.

Index fund investing

This strategy is for the investors that do not have the time required for researching the stocks viable for investment. Index fund investing lets an investor passively participate in the returns of the stock market. Moreover, this strategy is the only way that an investor can guarantee their share of the returns experienced by the stock market. Unlike mutual fund investing, it does not involve the costs of mutual funds – advisory fees, portfolio transaction fees, and operating expenses.

You can do index fund investing by buying shares in index funds or ETFs tracking market indices. This will already provide you a

Chapter 5: Stock Investing Strategies

diversified stock portfolio while assuring that your portfolio reflects the return of the stock market. You can further diversify your stock holdings by investing in indices of a different market, sector, country, or region.

Dollar-cost Averaging

Dollar cost averaging is an investment strategy of making regular investments in the stock market. It can be used in combination with other investing strategies. The premise behind dollar cost averaging is that fixed investments on a regular basis help investors avoid the temptation of timing the market. They are also purchasing in regular increments that result in a lower average on per-share cost. This method can be also be used in mutual funds and ETFs investing in the stock market.

Averaging down

This is an investment strategy wherein an investor purchases additional shares during downtrends. Like dollar-cost averaging, it can be used in conjunction with the other investment strategies. This works best in value investing, and stock dividend investing wherein the stocks are purchased with the long-term in mind. But, investors should be wary of averaging down on downtrends that arise from the loss of book value due to events or changes unaccounted for during your entry in the position.

Chapter 6: Principles of Trading in the Stock Market

Stock trading is the buying and selling of stocks to make quick profits. These profits are derived from market price movements of stock in the short term. Trading can also be done in other liquid markets like foreign currency trading, options, and futures.

Stock trading has a smaller margin realized due to the shorter holding period of stock. Because of this, it requires a higher trade volume for each position. An inadequate trading volume in a position would make it difficult to realize adequate profits for your endeavor. In some cases, a small trading volume could even result in a loss due to the fees due to your broker. Furthermore, stock trading involves executing stop-loss and limit orders to getting the best price for getting in or out of a position.

Best Practices in Stock trading

1. Always have a plan and stick to it

You have to set rules on what qualifies as a good point to enter or exit a position. You must also set the strategy and budget that you will follow for your trades. Having these will help remove the emotions and create consistency in your trades.

2. Do your research

Due to the short time frame of a trader holding their position, the economic and financial aspects of a stock do not play a role in trading decisions. Technical and statistical analyses are more significant, sometimes the only considerations in making trading decisions.

3. Treat it as a business

A business requires a commitment to succeed. This is the same for trading. Anything less would result in losses to a significant, if not whole, portion of your trading capital.

4. Be a continuous learner

Stock traders need to practice lifelong learning. They need to learn from the good and bad trades and see how they can improve upon it. They need to implement continuous improvements in their plant and test it before implementing it.

5. Protect your trading capital

Avoid unnecessary risks. Do your research for your trades and do it well. Let go of losing positions fast.

6. Do not risk what you can't afford to lose

The trading account should only contain funds that you can afford to lose. Do not put in funds allocated for personal expenses, the mortgage, your child's college tuition, and other personal expenses at any point in your trading career.

7. Always use a stop loss

Any position you enter should have a pre-planned stop-loss point set at the same time as your entry. With this set, losses from bad trades are taken into account ahead of time.

8. Know when to stop

If the plan is not working, you have to take a step back. Stop trading and see where it is going wrong. Do not return unless you have found out, and have created and tested a new trading plan.

This also applies if you are showing signs of being an ineffective trader. If you are unable to follow your plan, you have to pause and ask yourself if you can actually handle trading. This is also the case if you are experiencing personal problems or in bad health. You must always be at a good level in terms of mental, emotional, and physical health if you want to do well in stock trading.

Technical Analysis

Technical analysis is a discipline used to evaluate trading opportunities through the analysis of a stock's (or any security's) statistical trends. The data used to analyze a trend include the history of price movements, trading volume, and trading activity. Here are some of the indicators used in technical analysis:

1. Price trend

A price trend is a visual aid of two parallel lines illustrating the support line and resistance line of a stock's price movement. How the trend line slopes indicate the stock's current trend – it is an uptrend (bullish) if it slopes upwards while the opposite is true if it goes downwards. Whenever the stock price goes beyond the parallel lines, it is a sign of a possible new trend.

2. Chart patterns

These are formations formed over time on the price chart by the stock's market price. Recognizing these patterns formed can help you see possible price movements in the near future. Examples of chart patterns include pennant, cup and handle, top and inverse head and shoulders, ascending and descending triangle, triple bottom, rounding bottom, double top, and flag continuation. These are often used with the support and resistance lines of a stock's price trend.

3. Moving averages

This is the previous average of a stock over a given period. There are two types of moving average usually used – simple and exponential. Simple is the average with all previous stock prices given equal weight while the exponential moving average places greater importance for the more recent stock prices.

Moving averages are mostly used to determine good entry and exit points for a position. This is done by comparing the 50- and 200-day moving averages. When the 50-day goes above the 200-day moving average, it indicates an uptrend will occur in the short term. On the other hand, when the 50-day moving average goes below, a downtrend is expected to occur. The moving average is also used to see the actual trend amidst the price fluctuation present. A stock price consistently above the moving averages indicates a current uptrend. If it is at or below the moving averages, it indicates a downtrend.

4. Volume and momentum indicators

These give indications of the strength of an on-going trend and the chances of a change in trend (reversal). One of the momentum indicators in technical analysis is the average directional index (ADX). It determines if the current trend has an actual direction or if it is only a false signal. If the ADX indicates a value of below 25, the trend is directionless or just moving sideways. If it goes above 25, a trend exists, and the higher it goes indicates a stronger trend for a given stock.

Other indicators under this category include the Relative Strength Index (RSI), Stochastic, and Ichimoku Kinko Hyo.

5. Oscillators

It determines if a stock is overbought or oversold in the short-term. This is done by picking two extreme values of stock's price over a given period. Depending on the results, you will see where the trend is heading – a movement towards the higher value

Chapter 6: Principles of Trading in the Stock Market

means the stock is overbought while the opposite indicates an oversold stock.

Overbought stocks are those trading at a price above its book value, while oversold stocks are those trading below it.

Stock trading is not advisable for beginners in the stock market. Starting stock trading would often require months of study and practice in the stock market. The shorter timeframe between entering and exiting a position increases the likelihood of committing errors due to the greater impact of your emotions and external factors on your decision-making. Getting a handle of these require practical knowledge and some experience in, at least, investing in the stock market. In fact, some stock investors are not advised to trade stocks due to their aversion to the risks involved.

Chapter 7: Stock Trading Strategies

Stock trading uses short-term movements to profit from the stock market. The following are the different ways that stock traders use to take advantage of these movements:

Day Trading

This method involves buying and selling a position within the same day. There are no leftover positions once the trading hours are done for the day. This limitation helps traders limit their trading to stocks that can give them a reasonable return within the day. Also, it helps prevent losses on positions remaining at the end of the day.

This strategy requires a significant trading volume for each position to realize acceptable returns while covering for any fees in the transactions.

Position Trading

This is a strategy that involves the trader holding a position longer than the average trader. It could last from a day up to a month, depending on the trend. Position traders enter a position when a trend has already been established. They only exit a position when it breaks the current trend.

Chapter 7: Stock Trading Strategies

Swing Trading

This is a strategy that takes advantage of the increased volatility when a new trend is starting. It is the middle ground between day trading and position trading in terms of how long a position is held. Compared to the other strategies, it places a significant emphasis on fundamental analysis since it is crucial that large-cap stocks are chosen. These stocks have a high trading volume, which would provide a greater potential return.

Scalping

This strategy takes advantage of the price gaps created by the bid-ask spreads on a stock. This is done by entering the bid price and exiting at the asking price. Scalpers trade in liquid markets to increase their trade frequency since the strategy calls for taking advantage of small and frequent price movements. Furthermore, it works best in stocks that do not have sudden changes in market prices.

Chapter 8: Common Mistakes in Stock Investing and Trading

Investing or trading in the stock market is not easy. You will make mistakes that will cost you money. How much it would cost you would depend on how badly you make that mistake.

The first step to avoiding these mistakes is by knowing them. Here are some of the most common mistakes that people do when starting out in the stock market:

1. Poor Preparation

You need a plan when buying and selling shares in the stock market. If you are an investor, you need to know the stocks viable for your investment strategy even before you buy it. If you are a trader, preparing for your trade becomes even more important since, without a plan, you are essentially blind in the market.

Moreover, if you are new to the stock market, you need to prepare before you even start with your money. Read the basics about stocks and learn from the masters so you will have an easier time transitioning from a complete novice to a beginner. It would even help using a stock simulator so you at least know how to enter orders so you can do it right with your money.

2. Being Emotional

Greed, hope, and fear have no place in your decisions regarding the stock market. Having any of these is the recipe for veering away from your plan and sticking to a position that you should have already sold. It can even make you lose money regardless of the quality of your position.

To avoid this, you have to start trading small volumes in each stock. It might even help in starting with just a small capital and just add periodically through dollar cost averaging. In this way, each trade does not seem as big, and you are learning to detach your emotions from your stock positions.

3. No Recordkeeping

The key to long-term success in the stock market is continuous learning. You can only do this by improving what you do and learning from your mistakes.

To do this, you need to journal your premise behind your decisions. Record your actions in the market for the day. Write down your analysis and entry and exit points. You can even print out the charts you used and attach them to the corresponding journal entry so you have something to use as a basis when studying your journal.

In this way, you can see the improvements that you can make for better decisions in the future. You might even spot mistakes that you were not aware of.

4. Anticipating Returns

If you are anticipating potential returns, you are closing yourself off to the possibility that your stock positions could turn against you. This is a dangerous mindset to have since the conditions of a stock or the market can change. If this change occurs, whatever you know before is already inaccurate, and you need to adjust. And, this adjustment is hard to do if you set your mind up to think as if your returns are already realized.

5. Dependence on Tools

The tools are there to help you make better decisions. But, these tools cannot analyze the data and make the decisions for you. You still need to think if what these tools are telling you is actually relevant. These are not exempt from having limitations on how it can help you. You need to understand the different tools available to you and only use these in the right situations.

Knowing these common mistakes does not mean that you would not commit any of these in the future. After all, making mistakes in any endeavor is inevitable, and just how things go. But, knowing these mistakes makes you aware of what you could possibly do wrong. In this way, you are less likely to commit them. And, if you ever do, you would immediately recognize what you did wrong and take the appropriate actions to avoid it in the future.

Conclusion

I'd like to thank you and congratulate you on finishing this book.

I hope this book on the stock market was able to answer the questions running through your mind whenever it came up in the news, social media, or conversation. You now have an excellent foundation to get started and even look for a stockbroker that suits your needs. Of course, learning about the stock market does not stop here. If you really want to succeed, you would have to read more about it and, hopefully, start practicing with a stock market simulator. After that, hopefully, you have become more confident in getting started, open your first account with a stockbroker, and enter your first stock position.

I wish you the best of luck! Before we wrap up this book, I do have one favor to ask of you. Please take 2 minutes and write an honest review on the Amazon page.

Reviews are the lifeblood of our books and we would greatly appreciate your thoughts on it!

Thanks! Now, I think you will like the next page!

Bonus!

I'd like to thank you again for purchasing my book, so I want to give you a little gift.

Copy this link manually in any browser (It isn't too long):

https://mailchi.mp/ba1b6ac085da/blairpublishing

I hope it will be useful when you get started.

I wish you the best of luck!

Keep On!

Matthew Blair